Out of Maasai Land

sneh kotak

BookLeaf
Publishing

India | USA | UK

Presentation by *BookLeaf Publishing*

Web: www.bookleafpub.com

E-mail: info@bookleafpub.com

ISBN: 9789363317000

First edition 2024

to the vibrant lands and seas,

and to the hearts that beat within them.

and to nine year old me, full of wonder and glee,

you inspire me still, the essence of who i long to be.

ACKNOWLEDGEMENT

to all the wonderful souls who made Out of Maasai Land possible:

firstly, to my laptop for enduring countless keystrokes and late-night inspirations—your patience rivals that of a saint (or at least a very forgiving piece of technology).

to my family, who endured my ramblings with smiles and occasional eye rolls—you are the real MVPs. special shoutout to my sisters for always providing the best ribena and the most honest critiques.

and to my readers—thank you for embarking on this whimsical journey through cultures, seasons, and the unexpected twists of life.

may these poems bring you as much joy and laughter as they did to me while writing them.

PREFACE

dear reader,

welcome to Out of Maasai Land, where cultures collide in a poetic dance that's part laughter, part reflection, and wholly delightful. this collection of poems is like a lively gathering where Kenyan and Indian traditions mingle over chai and chapo.

we begin with childhood adventures—remember those days of making pies out of mud? (no? just me then? alright.) we tiptoe into deeper waters, contemplating life's mysteries with a twinkle in our eyes and a nod to the inevitable dance with death (things got serious).

amidst it all, we find the divine peeking through the everyday chaos, reminding us to pause and marvel. and of course, my favourite, the food! from simple khichdi to hearty ugali, each dish tells a tale served with warmth and love.

as the seasons change—from the whispering winds of enkare nyrobi to the suspended humidity of indian monsoon rains—each poem captures the essence of time's passage.

i invite you to savour life's flavours, share in its joys, and find solace in its shared moments. i hope these poems become your companion on through cultures, seasons, and the endless surprises of existence.

with heartfelt gratitude,

sneh

rainy road trips

in Enkare Nyrobi, mornings whispered cool and
clear,
each breath carried the scent of earth and dreams
we held dear.
on the schoolyard's canvas of mud, tales of
innocence were spun,
lost in childhood magic, under the African sun.

at the swimming pool, fear gripped tight, but
with Aamnah, laughter flowed,
Hannah Montana's tunes, our youthful hearts
bestowed.
beneath Mr. Cliff's guiding light, rules with
kindness were laid,
and Jeneby's Friday cola candies, sweet
memories never fade.

Mom's dosa, a taste of home, wrapped with
tender care,
library tales of fairies, in their enchanting lair,
on road trips to Kisumu, Nani's laughter filled
the air,
rain-soaked journeys, tears of joy, memories we
still share.

though time and years have passed, these
moments forever hold,
Kenya's childhood whispers, stories of pure
gold.

mursik memories

in home's embrace where the sun kissed the
savannah wide,
i savoured the flavours where Kenyan dishes
abide.
Mama's sukuma wiki, verdant greens that
danced on the tongue,
and pili pili ya kukaanga, spicy whispers that
flung.

in the kitchen's warmth, chapo swirled like the
African breeze,
a taste of tradition, wrapped in doughy embrace
with ease.
ugali, steadfast and strong, held memories in
each bite,
a comfort like no other, in the stillness of the
night.

amidst bustling markets, nyoyo simmered with
care,
their aroma, a promise of nourishment, flavours
rare.
maharagwe beans in coconut milk, a creamy
delight,

echoes of heritage in every morsel, pure and
bright.

in Westlands embrace, where memories stir and
intertwine,
these tastes of childhood linger, a banquet so
divine.
with every dish and every bite, a story unfolds
anew,
of love, of roots, of Kenya, where dreams and
flavours grew.

the garage

through the quiet corners of memory's keep,
i recall Nana where shadows softly meet.
his hands in the garage's care,
with oil and tyre scents, memories rare.

a bottle of White Cap, cigarettes in hand,
his smile, a beacon across the land.
in Tickly's garage, as a child i'd roam,
watching him work, feeling at home.

his morning prayers in the mandir light,
a ritual of faith, so gentle and right.
from Victoria's bakery, he'd return with glee,
baked goods shared lovingly, for all to see.

his laughter echoed, a melody so sweet,
his phrase "Welcome to the club" was a joy to
greet.
Nana, how i miss your presence here,
your laughter and wisdom forever near.

in the tapestry of my heart, your legacy's spun,
in nostalgia's embrace, till my own journey here
is done.

steeping stories

in gardens when the sun meets soil,
two kindred spirits brew and boil.
Kericho whispers in the dawn,
while Darjeeling sings till day is gone.

in Kericho's fields, the pickers roam,
with tender hands, they bring leaves home.
Darjeeling, high in mountain grace,
unfurls its petals in a race.

Kericho brews a deeper hue,
robust and rich, a Kenyan view.
Darjeeling's lighter, yet profound,
with floral notes that swirl around.

in cups they meet, their stories blend,
two cultures in a common trend.
tea soothes the weary, lifts the soul,
in steaming vessels, hearts are whole.

Kericho's warmth, a hug so tight,
revives the bones, restores the light.
while Darjeeling's calm, gentle embrace,
makes burdens lift, brings peace and grace.

rhythms above

across ancient halls where echoes sing,
divine the notes, as strings they ring.
veena's voice, Saraswati's grace,
a river flows from sound's embrace.

tabla's rhythm, Shiva's dance,
thunder beats, a cosmic dance.
flute of Krishna, soft and pure,
melodies that hearts allure.

sitar's whisper, gentle night,
stars aligned in raptured flight.
mridangam's pulse, Ganesha's might,
guardians of the sacred rite.

tanpura's hum, eternal drone,
a bridge to realms beyond our own.
each instrument, a voice, a prayer,
weaves a tapestry of air.

these timeless songs, their spirits wake,
through every note, the soul they take.
a tribute to the Gods above,
music's power, endless love.

language and legume

in the heart of Gujarat where flavours sing,
i find myself in dishes that memories bring.
the language speaks a melodious tune,
in kitchens alive, beneath the harvest moon.

thepla, with your fenugreek twist,
you whisper tales of fields and bliss.
khandvi, like rolled manuscripts of turmeric gold,
unfurls tales of traditions, bravely told.

dhokla rises, a sponge of gram and spice,
in morning's sight, a fragrant slice.
fafda's crunch, a savoury delight,
echoes of markets bustling late night.

as undhiyu simmers rich and slow,
it sings of winter bounty in rows.
shrikhand's sweetness- a saffron tinged tale,
of festive times and moonlit trails.

in many words, Gujarati unfolds,
a tapestry of stories, ancient and bold.
rhythms of prem and samaj, bright,
illuminate the velvet raatri night.

i am a part of spice and sanskriti,
in every dish, there's a dance of history.
for in the language, and in the feast,
i find myself, a soul released.

beyond greed

where endless plains stretch wild and free,
Maasai Mara, Voi, a sanctuary.
lions stride with regal pride,
elephants in ancient tide.

giraffes that brush the azure sky,
in their gaze, dreams soar high.
Kilimanjaro's icy crown,
in its shadow, peace is found.

through a rainy day car window,
Kericho's fields in shades of green glow,
raindrops trace on glass so clear,
a cool breeze whispers, drawing near.

the Big Five roam, their majesty clear,
in every shadow, every cheer.
Victoria's lake, serene and grand,
reflections dance on tranquil land.

Mombasa's coast, the ocean's song,
in beauty's simple, lasting throng.
yet, shadows linger where political power
sways,
the land more pure, untouched by figures astray.

from 254, where dreams take flight,
nature's gifts, both vast and bright,
could shine more brightly, free from fall,
in cherished realms, we find our all.

concrete or hay

city streets where sirens scream,
neon lights erase the dream,
a cacophony of restless noise,
where chaos reigns and calm destroys.

concrete canyons echo loud,
engines roar, a jarring shroud,
voices clash in frantic thrash,
a ceaseless, urban, relentless clash.

yet in the countryside's embrace,
silence wraps the rolling space.
whispers of the wind so light,
through ancient trees in velvet night.

stars emerge in tranquil skies,
no clamor to obscure their rise.
in stillness, peace and truth are found,
where nature's lullabies resound.

thus we wander, lost, entwined,
between discord and the kind,
seeking in the silence sweet,
a refuge from the city's beat.

the universe is a feather

in the meadow where peacocks dance,
a melody of divine romance,
flutes sing softly through the night,
bringing stars' celestial light.

whispers of a moonlit tale,
in forests deep, where shadows pale,
a figure plays flute, graceful, true,
in every leaf, a hint of blue.

radiance blinds the weary eye,
yet soothes the heart's longing sigh.
lotus blooms in sacred streams,
where heaven meets our earthly dreams.

with skin like midnight, deep and dark,
a presence leaving a radiant mark,
by his side, a beauty rare,
with ebony locks and skin so fair.

her grace, a sight to see,
in her, his heart finds harmony.
her eyes, like pools of endless love,
reflecting skies from up above.

in their depths, his solace lies,
her touch, the balm that never dies.
in dawn's soft light, their essence drawn,
a sacred love, forever shone.

Kanha's heart, incomplete alone,
in Radha's love, he finds his home.

cotton snakes

in shadowed groves where whispers coil,
a figure stands with gaze that spoils,
her eyes—a storm of hidden toil,
not born of malice, but of moil.

in Egypt's court and ancient lore,
a queen with grace and strength galore,
her power bright, a fierce encore,
both rise to inspire evermore.

"in silence, strength i must reclaim,"
she whispers to the stars' soft flame,
"no curse but power in my name,
 a truth beyond this endless blame."

their stories blend, both fierce and bold,
medusa's gaze and Cleopatra's hold—
in every woman's heart their truths unfold,
a legacy of strength retold.

shiny floors

in hallowed halls where shadows breed,
where power's lust sows discord's seed,
men in suits and women too,
their eyes alight with ruthless view.

politics, a somber game,
too grave for those who seek acclaim.
truth, though sharp and wise,
turns askew 'neath gilded skies.

shiny offices gleam with pride,
while refugee tents lie cast aside.
sacred values trampled, torn,
as empty promises adorn.

faiths are shattered by the chase,
in ruthless quests for power's grace.
a theater of masks and guise,
where honour fades and virtue dies.

serious business, cold and stark,
barters truth for fleeting mark.
beneath the weight of pomp and ploy,
sacred echoes, lost, deploy.

in the murk where shadows spin,
we grasp for truth beneath their din.
power's hunger, fierce and deep,
shall never stir the hearts we keep.

to a quill

in whispered tomes where shadows breathe,
a world shaped by the scribes beneath,
Shakespeare's stage of tempest's more,
in Macbeth, ambition's fierce uproar.

Sylvia Plath, with Bell Jar deep,
unveils the abyss where sorrows creep,
her lines like winter's biting chill,
a reflection of the struggle still.

Dostoevsky, with Crime and Punishment,
drew guilt's relentless, dark lament,
in Brothers Karamazov, we find
the chasms of the tortured mind.

Oscar Wilde's Picture of Dorian Gray,
a mirror to life's ironic sway,
his prose a dance of truth and guise,
where beauty and decay entwine.

Bronte's moors in Wuthering Heights,
unveil passions in storm-tossed nights,
her gothic tales of love's fierce plight,
turn shadows into piercing light.

through these pages, hearts are swayed,
their words, a world in ink arrayed,
each author's touch—a soul's refrain,
in every line, their legacies remain.

sugar, spice and languages nice

under gardens where the tongues of echoes
tread,
English tastes like buttered bread,
a warm embrace, a rustic, ancient fare,
a comfort in its simple, gentle air.

French, a sip of velvet wine, divine,
each word a golden drop, a sunlit sign,
while Spanish bursts like citrus bright and bold,
a vibrant dance in every story told.

Hindi swirls like spiced tea's fragrant grace,
a woven tale in every subtle taste,
Japanese whispers with refined art,
a matcha kiss that calms the restless heart.

Swahili sings of coconut's sweet cream,
a tropical delight, a sunlit dream,
Arabic's dates, rich honey's gentle might,
golden stories from the desert night.

Korean's kimchi offers piquant heat,
a tapestry where ancient echoes meet,

in every tongue and language, a world of taste to
find,
a universe where love and life is entwined.

gauze

in the quiet of my mind, I dwell,
where shadows cast their silent spell.
i, a girl of Gaza's pain,
dream of home through tears and rain.

i think of simple things I miss,
my mother's hug, a tender kiss.
the taste of bread, the taste of sugar,
living under a roof, feeling secure.

no pads for periods, a struggle so real,
in every ache, a silent appeal.
i long for school, to learn, to be,
someone with the power to set us free.

faces lost, whispers in the sand,
war has torn my cherished land.
anger burns, a fire deep inside,
at power's grip, and heartless pride.

home's a star in the night sky,
lit by hope, though shadows lie.
in every tear, a silent plea,
for our land that used to be.

i dream of a world where bombs don't fall,
where I have the strength to change it all.
to end the pain, the endless roam,
and bring us all back home,

back home.

dad

in twilight's hush, a Uniball pen rests calm,
its ink a tribute to a steady palm,
spectacles reflect a world through wisdom's
sheen,
holding silent tales of what might have been.

rap beats echo, his anthem's tune,
rhythms of struggle beneath the moon,
pizza's warmth speaks of shared delight,
a symbol of love that feels just right.

purple hues, deep and steadfast,
wrap our memories, a love that lasts,
in every detail, his care shines clear,
a constant strength we hold so dear.

through every slice and rap song's beat,
he's the guy who makes our lives complete,
in every moment, his love's our guide,
a funny, steady rock—our Dad,

our pride.

a cloaked friend

from twilight's whisper, where shadows meet,
lies a tale of quiet, in dreams we keep.
a friend when it comes, gentle and kind,
like being carried to your room, a child resigned.

laughter is heard from rooms nearby,
as these shadows dance beneath the sky.
not feared, nor dreaded but understood,
in life's hustle, where it concludes.

i hope for it to come as a gentle guide,
a soft sigh in the eventide,
like dusk descending calm and slow,
embracing my soul as twilight's glow.

no more to fear, no more to fight,
but peace and solace in fading light.
in the quiet moments as whispers wane,
i hope for its arrival to be serene and plain.

like childhood dreams, serene and deep,
in the twilight whispers, secrets we keep.
when laughter echoes and shadows blend,
i hope for it to come as a friend.

garden of privilege

in gardens of perception, where whispers bloom,
lies the tale of beauty, a comparison looms.
moths flutter by night's darkened mist,
neglected, unseen in the world's soft twist.

butterflies, bold in colours bright,
capture our gaze their beauty in flight.
petals embrace them, their place secure,
moths deemed unworthy, beauty obscure.

pretty privilege, subtle thief unseen,
steals the moth's admiration, bias keen.
muted wings, subtle hues defined,
grace eclipsed by privilege's design.

pause in gardens' hush profound,
seek beauty in moth wings unbound.
like butterflies, fragile in grace,
moths deserve our eyes' place.

dusk's soft glow, shadows lie,
cherish moths, let beauty amplify.
in twilight's gentle aim, let us hail,
every creature's beauty, its rightful claim.

veil of colours

in sun and shadow's tender play,
i walk where colours bend and sway.
a skin kissed by the savannah sun,
yet seen by some as not the one.

in these crowded streets, hearts should extend,
but whispers follow, hard to mend.
the hues i wear, earth's own mace,
viewed as strange, a hidden trace.

my heritage, a tale of seas,
whispers through the ancient trees.
yet here, where spices fill the air,
i face a world that doesn't care.

for in this dance of light and shade,
a harsh truth stands, cruelly made.
eyes that judge, words unkind,
leave silent cries within my mind.

in between lands where my cultures meet,
i bear the sting of bias' heat.

toys and time

from the gentle passage of childhood's embrace,
Diya, Shiv, Kirtan and Kian grow with grace.
toy cars raced on carpets, joyous uproar,
cartoon painted smiles, memories to store.

Diya my sweet, as you blossom and unfold,
let not worries weigh, let dreams take hold.
in your heart courage and laughter reside,
guiding you through a fun life's ride.

Shiv, Kirtan, Kian, my brothers sweet and true,
in kindness and love, i see reflections of you.
may your innocence shine, gentle and bright,
a beacon of warmth in life's twilight.

in shared laughter and cherished embrace,
in the tapestry of family, love finds its place.
to Diya, Shiv, Kirtan and Kian, my cherished
kin,
your smiles and dreams fill our lives within.

two shenanigans

in the whirlwind of giggles and tangled hair,
Jhanvi and Ashika are a duo quite rare.
one with a grin that could light up Times Square,
the other like a tsunami, chaos everywhere.

they scheme and they plot, with giggles so loud,
turning dull moments into adventures proud.
in socks mismatched and chatters so wild,
they navigate life, undefiled.

with marker masterpieces on any wall,
they paint our world, standing tall.
their jokes and antics, a daily delight,
making even the grumpiest days feel bright.

J's smile is like sunshine in May,
A's laughter making blues go away.
in your joy, my heart finds its beat,
through antics and mischief life is made sweet.

so here's to my partners in crime,
through laughter and mischief for all time.
in this comedy of life, you're my stars above,
forever cherished, with endless love.

an ode to her

from the quiet hours before dawn's soft light,
i ponder of mom's dreams, a steadfast sight.
from the moment of my newborn cry,
she raised me up without a sigh.

from zero to twenty, her gentle hand,
guided me through life's shifting sand.
her dreams for me, a tapestry so grand,
woven with love by her command.

in her eyes i see constellations gleam,
dreams that shimmer in life's gentle stream.
her heart a fortress, resilient and true,
in her dreams, my path she drew.

through laughter and tears she held me tight,
nurturing dreams both day and night.
mummy my cutie, your dreams unfold,
in every story yet untold.

these lines, a tribute from heart to heart,
to the one i look up to for a strong start.
proud i am of all you have achieved,
your strength and love, a gift received.

with hopeful eyes, i cherish your place,

mummy,

thank you for being my guiding star,
in life's endless race.